REAL WORLD
MATHS

C000135171

ZOO

yet

by Wendy Clemson, David Clemson,
and Ghislaine Sayers

**Tick
Tock**

An Hachette UK Company
www.hachette.co.uk
Copyright © Octopus Publishing Group Ltd 2013

First published in Great Britain in 2013 by
TickTock, an imprint of Octopus Publishing Group Ltd,
Endeavour House, 189 Shaftesbury Avenue, London WC2H 8JY.
www.octopusbooks.co.uk

A CIP record of this book is available from the British Library.

ISBN 978 1 84898 915 3

Printed and bound in China

10 9 8 7 6 5 4 3 2 1

With thanks to our consultants: Jenni Back and Liz Pumfrey from the NRICH Project,
Cambridge University, Kerry Johnson and Debra Voege.

Publisher's note: We have included the imperial measurements miles and mph,
as both are commonly used in some countries.

WENDY CLEMSON

Wendy is experienced in working with and for children, and has been writing full-time since 1989. Her publications, which now exceed one hundred, have been written for children and sometimes their parents and teachers. In her many maths books, the aim is always to present the reader with challenges that are fun to do.

DAVID CLEMSON

David has wide-ranging experience as a writer and educationalist. His publications list is prodigious. In collaboration with Wendy, David has worked on many maths books for children. He is fascinated by maths and logic puzzles and is keen for the reader to enjoy them too.

GHISLAINE SAYERS

Ghislaine began working with animals while still at school, helping on friends' farms and looking after her own pets. After taking her 'A' levels, Ghislaine studied veterinary science at university and at London Zoo. Ghislaine has worked both in a mixed veterinary practice and with wild animals in Africa. She is now the zoo vet at Paignton Zoo in Devon.

CONTENTS

NUMERACY WORK COVERED IN THIS BOOK:

CALCULATIONS:
Throughout this book there are opportunities to practise **addition, subtraction, multiplication** and **division** using both mental calculation strategies and pencil and paper methods.

NUMBERS AND THE NUMBER SYSTEM:
- DECIMALS: pg. 8
- ESTIMATING (using a number line): pg. 27
- FRACTIONS: pgs. 8, 26
- NUMBER SEQUENCES: pg. 14
- ORDERING NUMBERS: pgs. 16, 27
- PERCENTAGES: pg. 12

SOLVING 'REAL LIFE' PROBLEMS:
- MEASURES: pgs. 6, 8, 17, 18, 26
- MONEY: pgs. 24, 25
- TIME: pgs. 10, 11, 26

HANDLING DATA:
- BAR LINE CHARTS: pg. 22
- USING TABLES/CHARTS/DIAGRAMS: pgs. 6, 8, 10, 11, 12, 14, 16, 18, 21, 24, 27

MEASURES:
- AREA: pgs. 13, 21
- PERIMETER: pgs. 13, 20, 21
- RELATIONSHIPS BETWEEN UNITS OF MEASUREMENT: pg. 16
- SCALES (reading from scales): pg. 9
- USING METRIC/IMPERIAL MEASUREMENTS: pgs. 6, 8, 9, 13, 16, 17, 18, 20, 22, 26, 27
- VOCABULARY (time): pgs. 10, 11, 26, 27

SHAPE AND SPACE:
- 3-D SHAPES: pgs. 7, 13
- GRID CO-ORDINATES: pg. 23

Supports the maths work taught at Key Stage 2

HOW TO USE THIS BOOK

Maths is important in the lives of people everywhere. We use maths when we play a game, ride a bike, go shopping – in fact, all the time! Everyone needs to use maths at work. You may not realise it, but a zoo vet would use maths to care for an animal and even save its life! With this book you will get the chance to try lots of exciting maths activities using real life animal data and facts about the work of zoo vets. Practise your maths and numeracy skills and experience the thrill of what it's really like to be a busy zoo vet.

This exciting maths book is very easy to use – check out what's inside!

Fun to read information about animals and the work of zoo vets.

WORMING THE PRIMATES

All the animals at the zoo are wormed twice a year. Even if the faecal samples collected from an enclosure are negative, and do not show worm eggs, there may still be an animal in that enclosure with worms. The keepers might not have managed to collect faeces from that animal. All the animals in an enclosure are given powdered anthelmintics (worming drugs) in a small amount of food, when they are hungry. The vets can then check how much of the drug has been eaten. The rest of the animals' food is given afterwards. If an animal's test is positive, showing it has worms, that animal is wormed more frequently.

MATHS ACTIVITIES

Look for the **ZOO VET CASEBOOK.** You will find real life maths activities and questions to try.

To answer some of the questions, you will need to collect data from a DATA BOX. Sometimes, you will need to collect facts and data from the text or from charts and diagrams.

Be prepared! You will need a pen or pencil and a notebook for your workings and answers.

ZOO VET CASEBOOK

Each of the **primates** at the zoo needs to eat 50 **milligrams** of worming drug for every kilogram of their body weight. To work out the correct amount of drug to give to each animal, the zoo vet needs to know how much each of the animals weighs.

In the DATA BOX you will see the weights of the primates at the zoo. Use the data to compare them.
1) Which primate is the heaviest?
2) Which primate is the lightest?
3) Name an animal that is heavier than an adult male ring-tailed lemur, but lighter than an adult female colobus monkey
4) One of the primates and a crate weigh 3 kg. The crate weighs 2.6 kg when empty. Which of the primates is it?

ANIMAL CARE FACT

Sometimes drugs are given in foods that the animals are not normally allowed to eat – a bit like a bribe! The colobus monkeys, spider monkeys, Diana monkeys and swamp monkeys get their anthelmintic in mashed banana sandwiches. The gorillas and orang-utans have their worming drugs in a low sugar blackcurrant drink.

ANIMAL CARE FACT

How do you weigh a gorilla? In the gorillas' den there is a special platform with scales underneath. Food is put on the platform and the scales are zeroed. A gorilla is let into the enclosure. The gorilla sits on the platform to eat the food and can be weighed while it is eating.

A zoo vet examines a ring-tailed lemur.

16

Fun to read zoo vet facts.

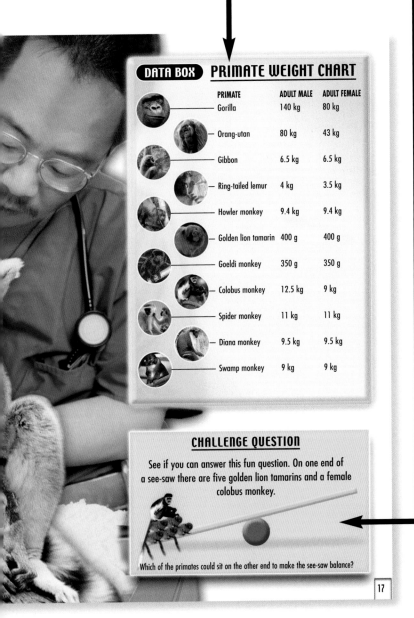

DATA BOX

If you see one of these boxes, there will be important data inside that will help you with the maths activities.

MATHS ACTIVITIES

Feeling confident? Try these extra **CHALLENGE QUESTIONS.**

DATA BOX   PRIMATE WEIGHT CHART

PRIMATE	ADULT MALE	ADULT FEMALE
Gorilla	140 kg	80 kg
Orang-utan	80 kg	43 kg
Gibbon	6.5 kg	6.5 kg
Ring-tailed lemur	4 kg	3.5 kg
Howler monkey	9.4 kg	9.4 kg
Golden lion tamarin	400 g	400 g
Goeldi monkey	350 g	350 g
Colobus monkey	12.5 kg	9 kg
Spider monkey	11 kg	11 kg
Diana monkey	9.5 kg	9.5 kg
Swamp monkey	9 kg	9 kg

CHALLENGE QUESTION

See if you can answer this fun question. On one end of a see-saw there are five golden lion tamarins and a female colobus monkey.

Which of the primates could sit on the other end to make the see-saw balance?

17

IF YOU NEED HELP...

TIPS FOR MATHS SUCCESS

On pages 28 – 29 you will find lots of tips to help you with your maths work.

ANSWERS

Turn to pages 30 – 31 to check your answers.
(Try all the activities and questions before you take a look at the answers.)

GLOSSARY

On page 32 there is a glossary of zoo vet words and a glossary of maths words. The glossary words appear **in bold** in the text.

5

ZOO VET TO THE RESCUE

Zoo vets work with wild animals from all over the world. Every day at work is different, and anything could happen! Your zoo has just received an emergency phone call from another zoo, hundreds of miles away. The other zoo has been flooded and their female giraffe, called Twizzle, urgently needs a new home. Your zoo has an enclosure for giraffes and a male giraffe who is waiting for a mate. You quickly agree that Twizzle can come to live at your zoo. First you will need to find a way to transport her. The zoo's lorry is big enough to carry Twizzle, but she will need to be inside a smaller travelling crate. The crate will have to be built as quickly as possible.

ZOO VET CASEBOOK

The zoo's maintenance crew have sketched out some designs for the giraffe's crate. All of the crates are made from panels that are strong enough to withstand Twizzle's kicks. Now you need to think about all her other needs:

- Twizzle must be able to sit down, stand up and turn around in her crate.

- The crate should have a roof made of netting or hessian (thick material).

- The crate must have ventilation (air holes). The ventilation holes must not allow Twizzle's horns to become stuck or be in a place where she can kick, as the crate will be weakened.

- The crate must be slightly higher than Twizzle.

Look at the six crate designs in the DATA BOX.

1) Which crate would you choose?
2) Why did you choose that crate? List your reasons.

(You will find a TIP to help you with these questions on page 28)

Twizzle in the paddock at her old home.

ANIMAL CARE FACT

The floor of the giraffe's crate must allow urine (wee) to drain away during the journey. A false floor is made for the crate from a metal grid. There will be a small gap between the grid and the bottom of the crate which will allow any wetness to drain away, keeping Twizzle clean and dry. The walls of the crate and the grid on the floor will be padded with rubber matting to protect Twizzle during the journey. The floor must be comfortable to lie on, too, so the rubber matting will be covered in a thick layer of straw.

Body length: 3.5 metres

GIRAFFE CRATE DESIGNS

a) *Metal crossbar roof*

4.0 m

4.0 m

3.5 m

b) *Solid metal roof*

4.0 m

All the crates have air holes.

3.8 m

6.0 m

c) *Solid wood roof*

4.0 m

6.5 m

3.0 m

d) *Netting roof*

4.0 m

4.5 m

3.5 m

e) *Hessian roof*

4.0 m

4.5 m

4.0 m

f) *No roof*

4.0 m

4.2 m

4.2 m

*Height:
4.2 metres*

*Weight:
800 kilograms*

CHALLENGE QUESTIONS

Here are some unusual crates that the zoo's maintenance crew are working on:

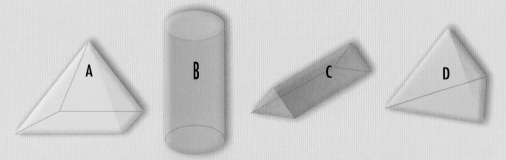

A   B   C   D

a) Match the name to the shape: cylinder, tetrahedron, square based pyramid, triangular **prism**.
b) Which two shapes have five **faces**? Which of these has five **vertices**?
c) Which shape has the fewest faces?

SEDATING A GIRAFFE

You have arrived to collect Twizzle from her old home, but first she will need to be given a **sedative** drug. The drug will make Twizzle feel calmer, and will ensure that she doesn't panic or hurt herself on the journey. Twizzle will be shut in her house and the sedative will be given by injection, using a dart shot from a dart gun. It is important that vets take their time and wait for exactly the right moment when darting an animal. If a vet misses with the first dart, an animal may panic. This makes it more difficult to get another shot. Before Twizzle can be darted, you will need to work out the correct amount of sedative to give her.

ZOO VET CASEBOOK

To work out the giraffe's drug dose you need to use **fractions** and **decimal fractions**.

1) Show what you know about how decimals and fractions are related by finding the missing numbers in this table:

?	1 ÷ 2	0.5
?	1 ÷ 4	?
?	?	0.75
$\frac{1}{10}$	?	?

2) What is one quarter of: 20, 80, 800?
3) What is one tenth of: 100, 50?

For every kilogram of her body weight, Twizzle needs 0.25 **milligrams** of sedative drug.

4) If Twizzle weighs 800 kg, how many mg of drug should we give her?
5) In each ml of injection there is 50 mg of drug. How many mls do you inject to sedate Twizzle?

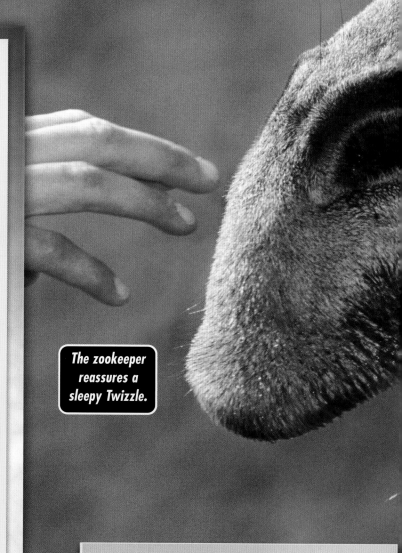

The zookeeper reassures a sleepy Twizzle.

ANIMAL CARE FACT

The sedative dart will eventually fall out of Twizzle as she walks around her enclosure, and her keepers will then retrieve it. During Twizzle's journey, it will be the vet's job to make sure she is in the best possible health. Giraffes are big, but they are timid, and can easily be startled by loud noises. Twizzle must be handled gently at all times.

CHALLENGE QUESTION

Test your skill at reading measuring scales.

How much medicine is in each container?

cl

ml
1000
900
800
700
600
500
400
300
200
100

a)

ml 15
10
5

b)

ml
0.1

c)

ml
150
100
50

d)

5
4
3
2
1

e)

(You will find information about UNITS OF MEASUREMENT on page 28)

ANIMAL CARE FACT

When a giraffe is darted, it sometimes panics and runs. The vets and zookeepers have to make sure that the enclosure is safe before they dart Twizzle. They check there are no sharp projections sticking out from the walls and remove the hay racks. The floor is covered in a deep layer of straw, so that it is not slippery.

TWIZZLE ON THE MOVE!

It takes 24 hours for the full effect of the **sedative** to work on Twizzle. The sedative will now keep her calm for approximately seven days. The next morning, when Twizzle is fully sedated, she is walked to the travelling crate. A pathway from the door of her enclosure to the back of the crate is walled with hessian (thick material) to stop her seeing anything that may worry or scare her. The keepers gently coax Twizzle into the crate, tempting her with her favourite food, branches with leaves. When Twizzle is inside the crate, it is gently winched onto the lorry. Twizzle is ready to go to her new home.

ZOO VET CASEBOOK

It is important to plan Twizzle's journey very carefully. She must be healthy and calm when she arrives at her new home.

- The lorry will need to travel quite slowly, so a short route must be chosen.
- The lorry will be very tall to carry Twizzle, so the route must avoid low bridges.
- Bendy roads must be avoided in case Twizzle topples over.
- Every three hours, the lorry must stop at the side of the road for 30 minutes so that Twizzle can be checked and given some food and water.

In the DATA BOX you will see three possible routes.

Each black space on the routes represents 30 minutes (½ hour) of travelling time.

1) Which route will give you the fastest journey time?

2) How long does the journey take?

(Don't forget that every three hours you need to add an extra 30 minutes for a checking and feeding stop. These are not shown on the route map.)

(You will find TIPS to help you with these questions on page 28)

ANIMAL CARE FACT

The driver of the lorry must be extremely careful when stopping, accelerating and turning, in case Twizzle falls over. The driver must also choose quiet places to stop, so that Twizzle is not scared by noises and people while she has her food and water.

GIRAFFE FACT

Giraffes usually sleep standing up because it takes them a long time to get to their feet if they are approached by a predator. Although Twizzle is safe from predators in her enclosure at the zoo, her **instincts** still tell her to do this.

Twizzle is gently tempted into the crate.

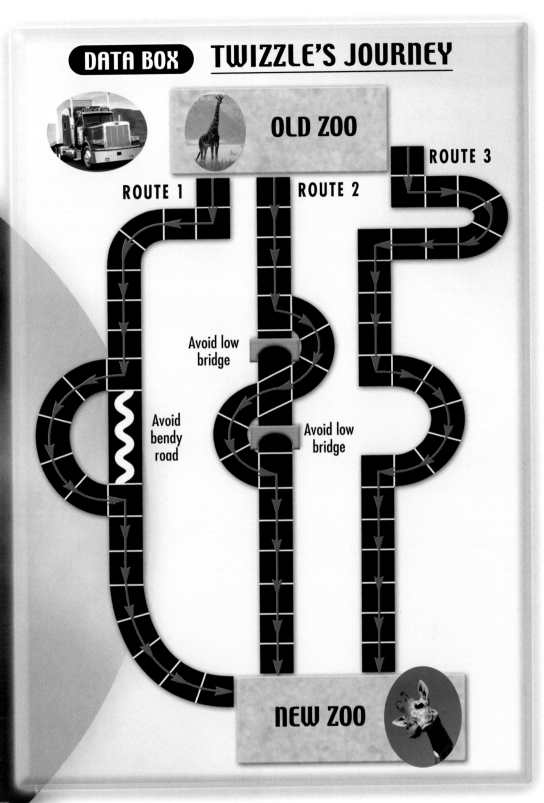

DATA BOX | **TWIZZLE'S JOURNEY**

OLD ZOO

ROUTE 1   ROUTE 2   ROUTE 3

Avoid low bridge

Avoid bendy road

Avoid low bridge

NEW ZOO

CHALLENGE QUESTIONS

Use the routes in the DATA BOX to answer these questions:

a) How many checking and feeding stops would you have to make if you used ROUTE 3?

b) If the lorry left the old zoo at 9:00 am and took ROUTE 2, what time would it be when the lorry stopped for Twizzle's second check-up?

c) Which route are you on if the total journey time is 750 minutes (including the checking and feeding stops)?

(You will find TIPS to help you with these questions on page 28)

A NEW HOME FOR TWIZZLE

When Twizzle arrives at her new home, she will need time to explore her surroundings and recover from the long journey. She will also want to find out which parts of her enclosure feel safe and where her food and water comes from. On arrival, Twizzle is coaxed from the crate and put inside the giraffe enclosure on her own. She can see and smell the male giraffe, but she will not be able to touch him for a few days. The keepers quietly watch over her, and give her lots of vegetables, fruit and browse (branches with leaves). These foods contain a large amount of water. It is very important that Twizzle feeds and takes in enough fluids.

ZOO VET CASEBOOK

Zoo vets have to work out exactly how much food an animal needs for good health.

In the DATA BOX you will see a chart that shows a giraffe's diet set down in hundredths. As you can see $^{15}/_{100}$ as a **fraction** of the diet is apples. This is 15 parts out of 100, or *15 percent*. The symbol for percent is %.

1) How much of the giraffe's diet is horse pellets?
2) What percentage is cabbage?
3) How much of the diet is apple and carrot added together?

(You will find help with using PERCENTAGES on page 28)

ANIMAL CARE FACT

Sometimes animals will not eat in new surroundings. Powdered glucose and electrolytes (sugars and salts) are added to their drinking water to give them some energy.

Twizzle settles into her new home.

- A few days after her arrival at the zoo, Twizzle and the male giraffe were allowed together for a couple of hours, while the keepers kept watch.
- When the keepers were satisfied that the two giraffes were getting on well, Twizzle was able to stay with her new mate all the time, but only inside the giraffe house.
- After a few more days, Twizzle and the male were let out and allowed to stay together in the outside enclosure.

DATA BOX) GIRAFFE DIET

- Horse pellets
- Browse concentrate
- Apples
- Carrots
- Cabbages
- Browse (branches)

CHALLENGE QUESTIONS

The keepers have been busy collecting straw bales to build Twizzle a comfortable bed. They use a small electric vehicle called a *gator* to drive around the zoo.

a) The gator is part full of straw bales. How many more bales will fill the gator, is it 16, 18, 8 or 14?

The straw bales are 2 metres long and 1 metre wide. Twizzle's bed needs to be 8 metres long and 6 metres wide.

b) How many bales are needed to build the bed?
c) If the bed only needs to be half a bale deep, the bales can be sliced in two. How many bales are needed then?

CHECKING FOR PARASITES

It is spring – time to test all the animals at the zoo for worms! **Parasitic** worms can harm the animals and cause diarrhoea and weight loss. The parasitic worms lay their eggs in the animals' guts, then the eggs are passed out in the animals' faeces (poo). The eggs lie on the ground, and when the animals eat the grass or plants in their enclosures, they sometimes also eat the worm eggs. The eggs then go back into the animals' stomachs and develop into more worms. All zoo animals need to be checked twice a year to make sure that the number of parasites doesn't build up inside them, making them ill.

ZOO VET CASEBOOK

Wearing gloves, the vets and keepers collect faeces from all the enclosures at the zoo, then they test the faeces to check for worms. The number of worms in an animal's stomach depends on how quickly new worms are born.

If the number of worms doubled every 4 weeks, we could make a table like this:

WEEKS	0	1	2	3	4	5	6	7	8	9	10	11	12
Number of worms if the number doubles every 4 weeks	1 WORM				2 WORMS				4 WORMS				8 WORMS

Can you see how this works? Now try to complete this table.

WEEKS	0	1	2	3	4	5	6	7	8	9	10	11	12
Number of worms if the number doubles every 3 weeks	1 WORM			2 WORMS			?			?			?
Every 2 weeks	1 WORM		2 WORMS		?		?		16 WORMS		?		?
Every week	1 WORM	2 WORMS	?	?	?	?	?	?	?	?	?	?	?

Toxocara worm eggs (from a cheetah) viewed through a microscope.

ZOO VET DIARY:
POO COLLECTION WEEK!

- Some enclosures at the zoo have a whole family of animals living there. A small amount of poo has to be collected from lots of different piles. Hopefully there will be some from each animal.

- Some worms don't lay eggs every day, so poo is collected for three consecutive days.

- In the zoo lab, each of the poo samples is tested. Water and 3 grams of poo from each sample is shaken up with glass beads which break up the poo.

- The liquid poo is then sieved. The microscopic worm eggs and water pass through the sieve and into a test tube.

- The test tube then goes into a centrifuge. This machine spins the tube and liquid very quickly and forces all the eggs to the bottom of the tube. The water is then tipped away.

- A special solution is added to make the eggs float. The eggs are then collected with a pipette, put on a glass slide and counted under a microscope.

CHALLENGE QUESTION

Cheetahs can have a parasitic worm called toxocara. A female toxocara worm can lay 700 eggs in each gram of cheetah faeces.

If a cheetah produces 800 grams of faeces in a day, and has one toxocara worm in its stomach, how many worm eggs will have been laid?

(You will find a TIP to help you with this question on page 28)

ANIMAL CARE FACT

Animals in zoos need to be wormed because they live in the same enclosures all the time and may eat grass or food contaminated by worm eggs. In the wild, animals move from place to place, so there is less chance of them eating worm eggs.

WORMING THE PRIMATES

All the animals at the zoo are wormed twice a year. Even if the faecal samples collected from an enclosure are negative, and do not show worm eggs, there may still be an animal in that enclosure with worms. The keepers might not have managed to collect faeces from that animal. All the animals in an enclosure are given powdered anthelmintics (worming drugs) in a small amount of food, when they are hungry. The vets can then check how much of the drug has been eaten. The rest of the animals' food is given afterwards. If an animal's test is positive, showing it has worms, that animal is wormed more frequently.

ZOO VET CASEBOOK

Each of the **primates** at the zoo needs to eat 50 **milligrams** of worming drug for every kilogram of their body weight. To work out the correct amount of drug to give to each animal, the zoo vet needs to know how much each of the animals weighs.

In the DATA BOX you will see the weights of the primates at the zoo.
Use the data to compare them.

1) Which primate is the heaviest?
2) Which primate is the lightest?
3) Name an animal that is heavier than an adult male ring-tailed lemur, but lighter than an adult female colobus monkey
4) One of the primates and a crate weigh 3 kg. The crate weighs 2.6 kg when empty. Which of the primates is it?

(You will find a TIP to help you with these questions on page 28)

A zoo vet examines a ring-tailed lemur.

ANIMAL CARE FACT

Sometimes drugs are given in foods that the animals are not normally allowed to eat – a bit like a bribe! The colobus monkeys, spider monkeys, Diana monkeys and swamp monkeys get their anthelmintic in mashed banana sandwiches. The gorillas and orang-utans have their worming drugs in a low sugar blackcurrant drink.

ANIMAL CARE FACT

How do you weigh a gorilla?
In the gorillas' den there is a special platform with scales underneath. Food is put on the platform and the scales are zeroed. A gorilla is let into the enclosure. The gorilla sits on the platform to eat the food and can be weighed while it is eating.

PRIMATE WEIGHT CHART

PRIMATE	ADULT MALE	ADULT FEMALE
Gorilla	140 kg	80 kg
Orang-utan	80 kg	43 kg
Gibbon	6.5 kg	6.5 kg
Ring-tailed lemur	4 kg	3.5 kg
Howler monkey	9.4 kg	9.4 kg
Golden lion tamarin	400 g	400 g
Goeldi monkey	350 g	350 g
Colobus monkey	12.5 kg	9 kg
Spider monkey	11 kg	11 kg
Diana monkey	9.5 kg	9.5 kg
Swamp monkey	9 kg	9 kg

CHALLENGE QUESTION

See if you can answer this fun question. On one end of a see-saw there are five golden lion tamarins and a female colobus monkey.

Which of the primates could sit on the other end to make the see-saw balance?

MEDICAL EMERGENCY: POISONING

You have just received an urgent message on your pager: one of the wolves is ill, he has collapsed, is having fits and is hardly breathing. When you get to "Wolf Wood", you see there is vomit in the enclosure. Wearing gloves, you poke through the vomit to see if you can find a clue to why the wolf is ill. The vomit smells very sweet and you find pieces of foil and a substance that looks suspiciously like chocolate. Someone has thrown their sweets into the wolves' enclosure. Many animals, including *canids* (the dog family), can be poisoned by chocolate. There is no cure – all a vet can do is support the animal while it tries to recover.

ZOO VET CASEBOOK

The wolf is placed in a large crate and rushed to the treatment room in the zoo hospital.

A catheter (a thin tube) is put into a vein in one of the wolf's front legs. The catheter is used to give drugs and fluids and to take blood samples for testing. The wolf needs to be given fluids to maintain his blood pressure and stop him going into shock.

1) Every hour the wolf is given 10 ml of fluids for every kilogram that he weighs. If the wolf weighs 30 kg, how many ml of fluids is he given each hour?
2) How many ml of fluids will the wolf be given in 1 minute?
3) If there are 20 drops of fluid in 1 ml, how many drops is the wolf given in 1 minute?

Wolf bites can be serious, so the wolf is given anaesthetic gas mixed with oxygen to keep him calm while he is being treated.

CHALLENGE QUESTIONS

Many animals have a specialised diet and can become very ill or overweight if they eat the wrong foods. Sometimes they can even die.

Study the food chart in the DATA BOX.

Which of the animals should eat: a) Grass b) Bread c) Chicken
Which of the animals must not eat: d) Chocolate e) Meat f) Boxwood g) Ragwort
h) For which of the animals might these food bowls be prepared?

Food bowl A

Food bowl B

Food bowl C

DATA BOX — FOOD CHART

NAME OF ANIMAL	FOODS FOR GOOD HEALTH							POISONOUS FOODS			
	GRASS	MAIZE	BREAD	CHICKEN	MEAT ON THE BONE	STRAW	VEGETABLES	MEAT	CHOCOLATE	BOXWOOD (PLANT)	RAGWORT (PLANT)
ELEPHANT		✓	✓			✓	✓	✓			
ASIATIC LION				✓	✓				✓		
ZEBRA	✓					✓				✓	
KANGAROO	✓		✓				✓				✓
WOLF				✓	✓				✓		

ZOO VET DIARY: SAVING THE WOLF

- When the wolf arrived in the zoo hospital, he was given oxygen (by mask) and his heart rate and rhythm were checked with a stethoscope. His temperature, respiration rate (breathing) and blood pressure were monitored at all times.

- Blood samples were sent straight to the lab for analysis. The wolf was given a drug to sedate him slightly and decrease the fits. Then he was given fluids.

- After four hours, the wolf started to improve, and he was moved to the recovery pens. During the night, the wolf was checked every three hours to make sure the fits hadn't started again.

- The next day, the wolf was given a small amount of high energy, easy-to-digest food. His medication was hidden in the food. A week later, the wolf was well enough to go back to his family.

ANIMAL CARE FACT

Visitors to zoos often throw their own food into the animals' enclosures. Sometimes visitors pick leaves from bushes growing outside the enclosure and throw these in, not knowing whether they are poisonous or not. Notices at zoos asking visitors not to feed the animals SHOULD NEVER BE IGNORED.

One of the vets prepares to treat the wolf.

THE RED RIVER HOGS MOVE IN

In a couple of weeks time there will be some more new arrivals. Preparations are under way to welcome three red river hogs who are moving from another zoo. Red river hogs are found in Africa and Madagascar, where they live wild in forests and warm, moist woodlands. Red river hogs spend a lot of time rooting in the soil with their noses, looking for food. They can soon turn a wooded area into a muddy field. The keepers have chosen a space for the hogs' enclosure where there is thick undergrowth and lots of trees. Now you need to help plan their new home.

ZOO VET CASEBOOK

There are lots of important safety precautions to remember when planning a zoo enclosure.

- The fence around the enclosure will go under the soil for 50 centimetres to prevent the hogs from digging out.
- The fence will be 1.5 metres high, to stop visitors leaning over.
- Around the edge of the enclosure there will be a *stand off* barrier. This extra barrier is 1 metre from the main fence, and it stops visitors putting their fingers through the main fence where they could receive a bite from a hog!

The hogs' enclosure will be a rectangle, 100 metres long and 42 metres wide.

1) What is the enclosure's **perimeter**?
2) If each fence panel is 4 metres wide, how many panels are needed?

(You will find a TIP to help you with question 1 on page 28)

ANIMAL CARE FACT

When the red river hogs arrive at the zoo they will go into their new enclosure over a weighbridge. The vet and keepers will then know how much each hog weighs. This information will be useful if the vet needs to give the hogs medication, or if the females become pregnant.

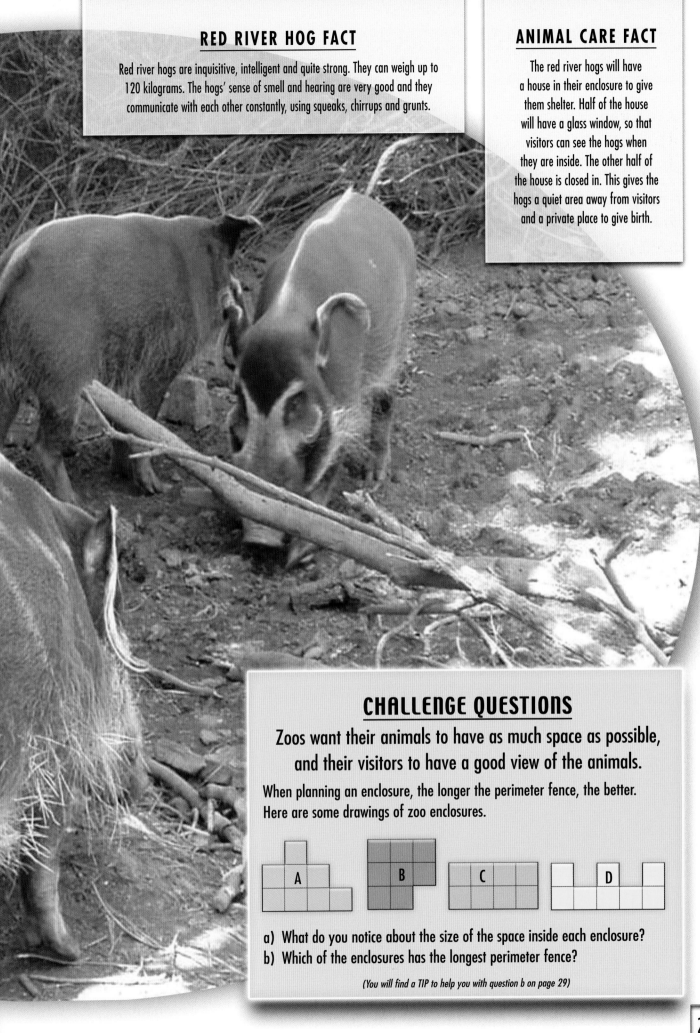

RED RIVER HOG FACT

Red river hogs are inquisitive, intelligent and quite strong. They can weigh up to 120 kilograms. The hogs' sense of smell and hearing are very good and they communicate with each other constantly, using squeaks, chirrups and grunts.

ANIMAL CARE FACT

The red river hogs will have a house in their enclosure to give them shelter. Half of the house will have a glass window, so that visitors can see the hogs when they are inside. The other half of the house is closed in. This gives the hogs a quiet area away from visitors and a private place to give birth.

CHALLENGE QUESTIONS

Zoos want their animals to have as much space as possible, and their visitors to have a good view of the animals.

When planning an enclosure, the longer the perimeter fence, the better. Here are some drawings of zoo enclosures.

A   B   C   D

a) What do you notice about the size of the space inside each enclosure?
b) Which of the enclosures has the longest perimeter fence?

(You will find a TIP to help you with question b on page 29)

AMELIA'S DIET

The red river hogs have settled into their new home. However, one of the hogs, Amelia, is losing weight. There could be lots of reasons why Amelia is getting thinner. She may have a painful mouth or a rotten tooth, the keepers may not be feeding the hogs enough or Amelia might have worms. You talk through the problem with the hogs' keeper, but there are no clues. When you visit the hogs' enclosure at feeding time, you notice that the two fatter pigs keep chasing Amelia away from the food. Although Amelia is thin, she doesn't seem ill and is still bright, alert and active. You decide Amelia will be given more food and her weight will be monitored.

ZOO VET CASEBOOK

Each day at feeding time, Amelia is shut in the house to eat on her own. She is also given extra food. Some scales are put in the hogs' house and sometimes Amelia is given her food up on the scales, so her weight can be checked while she is busy eating.

Now Amelia has enough food all to herself, she starts to steadily gain weight. This *bar line graph* shows Amelia's weight over several weeks.

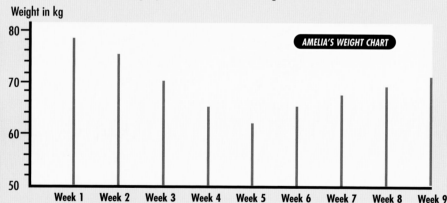

Amelia's healthy weight is shown in week 1.

1) What is Amelia's healthy weight?
2) For how many weeks does Amelia lose weight?
3) How much weight does Amelia gain from week 5 to week 6?
4) In weeks 7, 8 and 9, Amelia gains weight at a steady rate. How do we know this?
5) If Amelia goes on gaining weight at a steady rate, how many more weeks will it take to nearly reach her healthy weight?

(You will find information about BAR LINE GRAPHS on page 29)

RED RIVER HOG FACT

In the wild, red river hogs feed on a wide range of plant material, such as fungi, ferns, grasses, leaves, roots, bulbs and fruits. They also eat insect larvae, frogs, mice and earthworms. In the zoo, the hogs eat apples, bananas, carrots, cabbage, lettuce, bread and tomatoes. They are also given vitamins, pelleted food and chicks, for protein.

ANIMAL CARE FACT

When the hogs first moved into their new home they were getting a huge amount of food by eating the plants in their enclosure. Now the plants have all been eaten, the hogs' food will be increased by 50%. The food is also spread around the whole enclosure so that each hog has a chance to find food without being bullied by the others. Searching for food also gives the hogs more to do during the day.

CHALLENGE QUESTION

The edge of this grid is the fence around the hogs' enclosure. Food has been placed at (1, 2) and (3, 1).

At what other co-ordinates can food be placed away from the fence?

(You will find a TIP to help you with this question on page 29)

MONEY MATTERS

Many species of wild animals are **endangered** because humans are hunting them illegally or destroying their natural habitats. Lots of zoos around the world are now involved with important **conservation** and **research work.** These zoos give endangered animals a safe place to live. The zoos also run **breeding programmes** and they study the animals to find ways to help them in the wild. However, it costs hundreds of thousands of pounds each year to run a zoo, with lots of bills to be paid – food, medical care, heating and wages. Zoos raise the funds to pay for their work in many different ways – donations, entrance fees, animal adoptions and gift shops.

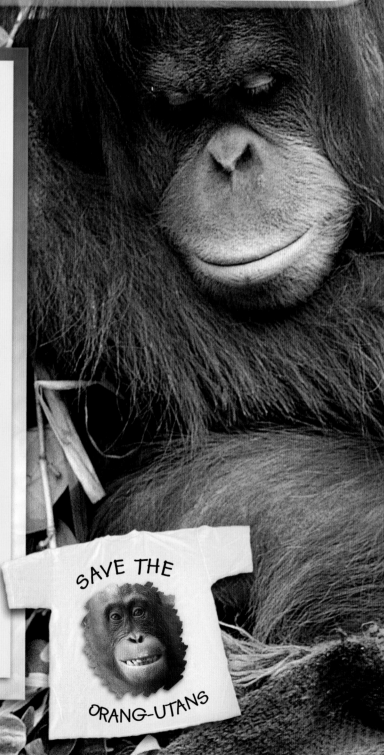

ZOO VET CASEBOOK

Zoo shops sell lots of fun gifts to their visitors. The profits the zoos make in their gift shops help to pay for the care of the animals.

Use the gift shop price list in the DATA BOX to help you answer these money questions.

1) What is the total cost of an orang-utan T-shirt and a zebra soft toy?
2) A visitor pays for a giraffe soft toy with two £1 coins and three 20p coins. How much change does she get?
3) If you buy a lion baseball cap, what change will you get from a £10 note?
4) How many postcards can be bought for £1.60?
5) Which of these can be bought for less than £9?
   • A pencil case and a set of three ballpoint pens.
   • A gorilla soft toy and a zebra soft toy.
   • A notebook and a flamingo soft toy.
6) A visitor puts these coins into the zoo fund collecting box: two 20p coins, three 50p coins, five 10p coins, four 5p coins and eight 2p coins. How much is that altogether?

(You will find TIPS to help you with these questions on page 29)

SAVE THE ORANG-UTANS

DATA BOX GIFT SHOP PRICE LIST

Ballpoint pens (set of three)	£ 3.00
Flamingo soft toy	£ 7.99
Giraffe soft toy	£ 2.50
Orang-utan T-shirt	£10.95
Lion baseball cap	£ 3.95
Notebook	£ 3.75
Gorilla soft toy	£ 4.00
Pencil case	£ 3.50
Postcard	20p
Zebra soft toy	£ 4.99

A baby orang-utan born in the zoo. Orang-utans are critically endangered. There are fewer than 25,000 left in the world!

CHALLENGE QUESTIONS

Many zoos run adoption schemes where you can pay a sum of money to adopt an animal. You don't get to take the animal home, but your money will help to pay for the animal's food and medical care.

Here are some adoption rates at the zoo:
- £1.50 a year for a llama.
- £2.75 a year for a hippopotamus.
- £5.25 a year for an elephant.

a) If you had £5, for how long could you adopt a llama?

b) If you had £5, for how long could you adopt a hippopotamus?

c) If you had £20, which animals could you adopt and for how long?

A baby African elephant born at the zoo.

TWIZZLE HAS A BABY!

Nearly two years have passed since Twizzle arrived at the zoo, and this morning she has given birth to a calf. However, from the moment the calf was born, Twizzle has ignored her baby, and her keepers are now very worried. The calf is taking his first faltering steps, but he isn't suckling and Twizzle is starting to become aggressive towards him. It is decided that the calf will be taken from Twizzle for his own safety. A mother's milk and **colostrum** are the best food for a newborn animal, but Twizzle is a first-time mum, and she doesn't seem to know what to do. Hopefully next time Twizzle has a baby, she will be a better mum.

ZOO VET CASEBOOK

Twizzle is let out of the calving pen and the keepers catch the calf to feed him. For the first few days, the baby will need to be fed colostrum, from a bottle, six times a day. After a few days, the colostrum will be replaced by milk.

On day 1, the calf has six feeds starting at 6:00 am and finishing at 9:00 pm.

1) If the feeds are evenly spaced throughout the day, at what times is the calf fed?

On day 1, the calf weighs 60 kg.

2) The calf is fed one tenth of his weight. How much is that?

3) How much food is the calf given at each feed?

4) If the calf only eats half of the food each time, how much food does he eat at each feed?

5) Next day, the calf eats three quarters of the food each time he is fed. How much food is that at each feed?

ANIMAL CARE FACT

Giraffes have a **gestation period** of 15 to 16 months. Elephants have the longest gestation period of any mammal, about 22 months – that's nearly two years!

Bottle-feeding the calf.

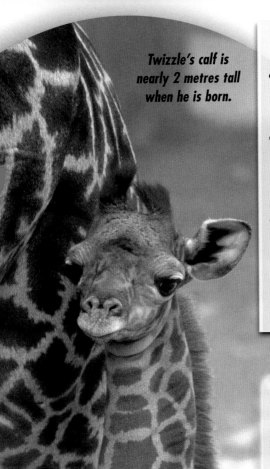

Twizzle's calf is nearly 2 metres tall when he is born.

ZOO VET DIARY: TWIZZLE'S CALF

- When Twizzle was about to give birth, her udders started to produce milk and swell up.
- Twizzle was separated from her mate and video cameras were set up in the enclosure so that her keepers could watch her without disturbing her.
- One morning, Twizzle began pacing up and down and she was not interested in her food. Later that day she gave birth.
- Like most giraffes, Twizzle gave birth standing up and her calf dropped onto the straw on the floor of the enclosure. However, Twizzle was completely disinterested in her calf and walked away.
- The keepers are now hand-rearing Twizzle's baby. After each feed, the keepers have to make the calf urinate and pass faeces by wiping his bottom with a damp cloth. Normally his mother would do this with her tongue.

DATA BOX ZOO BABIES

ANIMAL	GESTATION PERIOD	WEIGHT AT BIRTH
GIRAFFE	15 months	60 kg
RED RIVER HOG	120-127 days	0.75 kg
PANDA	45 days	100 g
RING-TAILED LEMUR	134 days	50 g
ELEPHANT	22 months	90 kg
GORILLA	8.5 months	2000 g
LION	14-15 weeks	1.5 kg
MOUSE	21 days	1.25 g
GIANT ANTEATER	190 days	1.25 kg
MALAYAN TAPIR	13 months	10 kg
GREY WOLF	63 days	0.5 kg
MOUNTAIN ZEBRA	12 months	25 kg

CHALLENGE QUESTIONS

Zoo vets need to be able to work out when animals will have their babies.

a) It is March and five animals at the zoo have become pregnant. The timeline shows when the five babies will be born. Work out what type of animal each of the babies is by using the information about gestation periods in the DATA BOX.

Baby A   Baby B   Baby C   Baby D   Baby E

March   May   June   October   March

b) Put all the animals in the DATA BOX in order of their birth weight, starting with the heaviest.

(You will find TIPS to help you with these questions on page 29)

TIPS FOR MATHS SUCCESS

PAGES 6–7

ZOO VET CASEBOOK

Handling data:

TIP: You need to ask these questions about each crate:

- Is the crate tall enough?
- All of the crates are 4 metres deep, but is the crate wide enough for the length of Twizzle's body?
- What is the roof made of?

PAGES 8–9

Units of measurement:

We use two systems of measurement in the UK: *metric* (centimetres, metres, kilometres, grams, kilograms) and *imperial* (inches, feet, miles, ounces, pounds).

METRIC		IMPERIAL	
Length		**Length**	
1 millimetre (mm)		1 inch (in)	
1 centimetre (cm)	= 10 mm	1 foot (ft)	= 12 in
1 metre (m)	= 100 cm	1 yard (yd)	= 3 ft
1 kilometre (km)	= 1000 m	1 mile	= 1760 yd
Weight		**Weight**	
1 gram (g)		1 ounce (oz)	
1 kilogram (kg)	= 1000 g	1 pound (lb)	= 16 oz
Capacity		**Capacity**	
1 millilitre (ml)		1 fluid ounce (fl oz)	
1 centilitre (cl) = 10 ml		1 UK pint (pt)	= 20 fl oz
1 litre (l) = 1000 ml		1 UK gallon (gal)	= 8 pt

Comparing metric and imperial measurements:

1 kilometre = 0.62 of a mile
1 kilogram = 2.2 pounds
0.57 litre = 1 UK pint

PAGES 10–11

ZOO VET CASEBOOK

TIP: There are many good ways to work out how long the journeys will take. One method is to count the spaces on each route in twos (two spaces = 1 hour travelling time). Then divide that total by three to give the number of half hour breaks to add. Remember, there are 60 minutes in one hour.

PAGES 12–13

ZOO VET CASEBOOK

Using percentages:

Percent is a special form of a **fraction** and means *'part of 100'*. For example: 50% is $^{50}/_{100}$ and 25% is $^{25}/_{100}$. Percentages are very useful for comparing amounts. They are often used in shops when prices are lowered in a sale. If an item costs £1.00 you might see: 50% OFF – this means the item now costs 50p.

PAGES 14–15

CHALLENGE QUESTION

Multiplication:

When multiplying hundreds, for example 200 x 300, try this method: multiply 2 x 3 to give 6, then look at the total number of zeros in 200 and 300. There are four zeros, so your answer is 60 000.

Check your answer with: 2 x 300 = 600
20 x 300 = 6000   200 x 300 = 60 000

PAGES 16–17

ZOO VET CASEBOOK

Using units of measurement:

TIP: When you are given measurements in mixed units it can be helpful to convert them all to the same unit so that they can be compared or used in calculations.

For example, 6.5 kg and 400 g can be compared as 6500 g and 400 g or as 6.5 kg and 0.4 kg.

PAGES 20–21

ZOO VET CASEBOOK

Measuring perimeter:

TIP: With rectangles you can work out the **perimeter** in three different ways:

- Add all four sides.
- Add one long and one short side and then double the answer.
- Double the length of the long side then double the length of the short side and add the totals together.

5 m
3 m — *3 m*
5 m

For example, the perimeter of this rectangle is 16 m.

CHALLENGE QUESTION

Measuring perimeter and area:

TIP: To find the **perimeter** of the enclosures, you can count the outer edges of the squares along the outside of each shape. We call the space inside the shapes the **AREA**.

ZOO VET CASEBOOK

Interpreting a bar line graph:

The chart on page 22 is known as a *bar line graph*. In this case we could connect the tops of the lines to make a continuous line graph. The left hand side does not start at 0 kg for two reasons: a hog will never weigh 0 kg, and starting at 50 kg makes the graph clearer.

CHALLENGE QUESTION

Using co-ordinates:

To find the co-ordinates of a point on a grid, you read along the bottom of the grid first, then up the side of the grid.

For example, a grid reference of **(3,2)** means **3 steps** along the bottom then **2 steps** up to find the exact spot.

ZOO VET CASEBOOK

Solving word problems involving money:

When doing shopping calculations, you can round up prices to work out approximate amounts. So £3.99 can be rounded to £4 to make mental work easier. Don't forget to take away 1p off the £4 to get the answer at the end!

Counting up helps us to calculate our change: If an item costs £4.95, and we pay with a £10 note, we can say, *'four pounds ninety five pence plus five pence equals five pounds'* and *'five pounds plus five pounds equals ten pounds'*, so the change is *'five pence plus five pounds'* which is £5.05.

CHALLENGE QUESTIONS

Measuring time using a number line:

A timeline is a kind of number line. Number lines are continuous and reach forever in both directions. We can make number lines to help in understanding and working with numbers.

This is a timeline

March   April   May

This is also a timeline

1   2   3   4   5
March

TIP: When you are given periods of time or measurements in mixed units it can be helpful to convert them all to the same unit so that they can be compared. There are:

- 7 days in one week.
- 4 to 5 weeks in one month.
- 12 months or 52 weeks in one year.

(You can use a calendar to find out the exact number of days in each month.)

29

PAGES 6-7

ZOO VET CASEBOOK

1) Crate e.
2) Crate e is the most suitable for Twizzle because:
   - The crate is taller than Twizzle, but not too tall.
   - The crate is big enough that Twizzle has room to turn around (her body is 3.5 metres long).
   - The crate has a hessian roof.

CHALLENGE QUESTIONS

a) The names of the shapes are:

A: Square based pyramid

B: Cylinder

C: Triangular prism

D: Tetrahedron

b) The square based pyramid and triangular **prism** have five **faces**. The square based pyramid has five **vertices**.

c) The cylinder has the fewest faces. Two circular faces and a curved surface along the length.

PAGES 8-9

ZOO VET CASEBOOK

1) The completed table should look like this:

½	1 ÷ 2	0.5
¼	1 ÷ 4	0.25
¾	3 ÷ 4	0.75
¹⁄₁₀	1 ÷ 10	0.1

2) One quarter of 20 is 5, 80 is 20, 800 is 200.
3) One tenth of 100 is 10, one tenth of 50 is 5.
4) Twizzle should be given 200 mg of drug.
5) We need to inject 4 ml to sedate Twizzle.

PAGES 8-9 continued

CHALLENGE QUESTION

a) 250 ml

b) 10 ml

c) 0.5 ml

d) 75 ml

e) 4 cl

PAGES 10-11

ZOO VET CASEBOOK

1) Route 2 gives the fastest journey time.
2) It will take 11 hours to reach the new zoo (9.5 hours travelling and three stops of 30 minutes each).

CHALLENGE QUESTIONS

a) You would make 4 checking and feeding stops.
b) Twizzle's second check-up would start at 3:30 pm.
c) Route 1.

PAGES 12-13

ZOO VET CASEBOOK

1) 20% (or ⅕) of the diet is horse pellets.
2) 10% (or ¹⁄₁₀) of the diet is cabbage.
3) 30% of the diet is apple and carrot added together.

CHALLENGE QUESTIONS

a) 14 more bales will fill the *gator*.
b) 24 bales are needed to build Twizzle's bed.
c) 12 bales are needed if they are sliced in two.

ANSWERS

PAGES 14–15

ZOO VET CASEBOOK

The completed table should look like this:

WEEKS	0	1	2	3	4	5	6	7	8	9	10	11	12
Number of worms if the number of worms doubles every 3 weeks	1 WORM			2 WORMS			4			8			16
Every 2 weeks	1 WORM		2 WORMS		4		8		16 WORMS		32		64
Every week	1 WORM	2 WORMS	4	8	16	32	64	128	256	512	1024	2048	4096

CHALLENGE QUESTION

Answer: 560 000 worm eggs!

PAGES 16–17

ZOO VET CASEBOOK

1) The adult male gorilla is the heaviest (140 kg).
2) The Goeldi monkeys are the lightest (350 g).
3) An adult male or female gibbon is heavier than an adult male ring-tailed lemur, but lighter than an adult female colobus monkey.
4) A golden lion tamarin (0.4 kg) and a crate (2.6 kg) will weigh 3 kg.

CHALLENGE QUESTION

A spider monkey would balance the see-saw!

PAGES 18–19

ZOO VET CASEBOOK

1) 300 ml   2) 5 ml   3) 100 drops

CHALLENGE QUESTIONS

a) Grass: zebra and kangaroo
b) Bread: elephant and kangaroo
c) Chicken: Asiatic lion and wolf
d) Chocolate: Asiatic lion and wolf
e) Meat: elephant
f) Boxwood: zebra
g) Ragwort: kangaroo
h) Food bowl A (chicken): Asiatic lion and wolf
   Food bowl B (vegetables): elephant and kangaroo
   Food bowl C (straw): elephant and zebra

PAGES 20–21

ZOO VET CASEBOOK

1) The enclosure's **perimeter** is 284 metres.
2) 71 fence panels are needed.

CHALLENGE QUESTIONS

a) The space inside each enclosure is the same.
b) Enclosure D has the longest perimeter fence.

PAGES 22–23

ZOO VET CASEBOOK

1) 78 kg   2) 4 weeks   3) 3 kg
4) Because the bar lines go up the same amount each week (2 kg).
5) 3 weeks

CHALLENGE QUESTION

Food can be placed at (1,1), (2,1), (2,2), (3,2)

PAGES 24–25

ZOO VET CASEBOOK

1) £15.94   2) 10p   3) £6.05   4) 8 postcards
5) A pencil case and a set of three ballpoint pens (£6.50)
   A gorilla and a zebra soft toy (£8.99)   6) £2.76

CHALLENGE QUESTIONS

a) 3 years (£4.50)   b) 1 year (£2.75)
c) A llama for 13 years (£19.50), a hippopotamus for 7 years (£19.25) or an elephant for 3 years (£15.75). (You could also adopt all three animals for 2 years.)

PAGES 26–27

ZOO VET CASEBOOK

1) The calf is fed at 6:00 am, 9:00 am, 12:00 pm (noon), 3:00 pm, 6:00 pm, 9:00 pm.
2) 6 kg   3) 1 kg   4) ½ kg or 500 g   5) ¾ kg or 750 g

CHALLENGE QUESTIONS

a) • Baby A is a grey wolf   • Baby B is a lion
   • Baby C is a giant anteater   • Baby D is a gorilla
   • Baby E is a mountain zebra
b) Elephant, giraffe, mountain zebra, Malayan tapir, gorilla, lion, giant anteater, red river hog, grey wolf, panda, ring-tailed lemur, mouse

GLOSSARY

BREEDING PROGRAMMES Zoos around the world work together to match up animals for breeding. If a species (type of animal) dies out in the wild, there will hopefully be a large and healthy population of that animal living in zoos. This will help to ensure that the species does not become extinct.

COLOSTRUM The first food produced by a mother to feed her baby. Colostrum is very nutritious (good for the baby) and contains antibodies, which kill germs and viruses.

CONSERVATION WORK Educating zoo visitors about wild animals, breeding endangered species and taking part in research to understand how best to look after and protect wild animals.

ENDANGERED When a population of animals is growing smaller due to hunting or loss of habitat. Eventually the animals may become extinct.

GESTATION PERIOD The length of time that an animal or human is pregnant.

INSTINCTS Ways of acting that are natural to an animal. The animal has never been taught to act in this way, but has inherited its response to particular situations from its ancestors.

PARASITIC When an organism (a living thing) lives in, or on, the body of another organism. For example, parasitic worms living in the stomachs of animals.

PRIMATES An animal group that includes monkeys, apes and prosimians (animals such as lemurs). Humans are primates, too.

RESEARCH WORK Zoos study ways to give zoo animals an environment to live in that is as close as possible to their natural home. Zoos study feeding, disease and reproduction. If zoo animals are happy and healthy, they are more likely to breed.

SEDATIVE A drug used to calm an animal or person. It can make the person or animal feel sleepy.

MATHS GLOSSARY

AREA The measure of the size of a surface, made in squares (all of the same size).

DECIMAL FRACTIONS We use a counting system involving tens, multiples of ten and fractions of ten. The decimal point separates whole numbers from decimal fractions. *For example, in the number 672.53, 5 is tenths and 3 is hundredths.*

FACES The flat surfaces of solid shapes.

FRACTIONS These are made when shapes or numbers are cut into equal parts. For example, if a shape is cut into four equal parts, each part is one whole divided by four, or a quarter (¼).

MILLIGRAM (mg) A unit of measurement. There are 1000 mg in one gram.

PERIMETER The distance all the way around a shape.

PRISM A solid shape the same size and shape all along its length. If you slice through a prism parallel to its end face, the cut faces will be the same size and shape as the ends. All the faces of a prism are flat (plane) and have three or more sides.

VERTICES These are corner points of flat (plane) shapes or 3-D shapes. For example, a cube has eight vertices.

t=top, b=bottom, c=centre, l=left, r=right, OFC=outside front cover, OBC=outside back cover

Alamy: 8-9, 10, 12-13, 18-19, 27, OBC.
Corbis: 2-3, 17, 24-25, 29tl, 29tc. Paignton Zoo: 20-21, 22-23, 26.
Photodisc: OFC, 1, 6-7, 11, 14-15, 17. Ticktock Media: 16-17main, 29br.

Every effort has been made to trace the copyright holders, and we apologize in advance for any unintentional omissions.
We would be pleased to insert the appropriate acknowledgements in any subsequent edition of this publication.